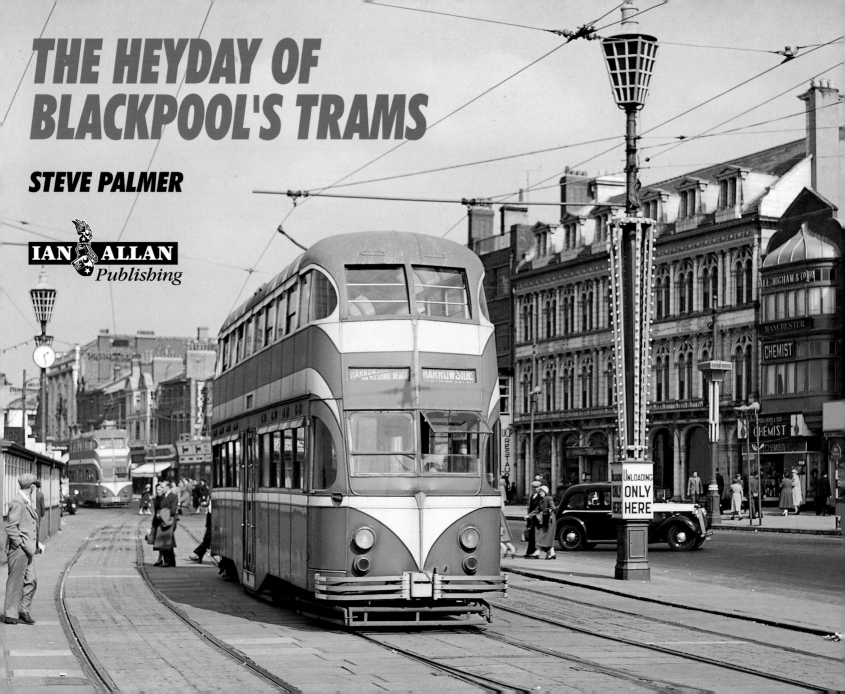

THE HEYDAY OF BLACKPOOL'S TRAMS

STEVE PALMER

IAN ALLAN Publishing

Contents

Introduction	2
Features of the 1950s	3
The 75th Anniversary — 1960	20
Sights of the Sixties	25
Illuminated Trams	50
Look Out — Trams About	54
The Age of the 1980s	64

Front cover: 'Standard' No 160 on 28 February 1965, posing to establish that Blackpool's heyday has featured trams on Central Promenade since 1885 and the Tower since 1894, making this the Golden Mile. *Steve Palmer*

Back Cover, main picture: Balcony 'Standard' No 40 in August 1985, depicting the tremendous enjoyment for everybody riding along the Promenade on this tram in the evening sunshine. *Steve Palmer*

Back cover, left: Central Promenade in 1963, with the vintage 'Dreadnought' giving popular rides in the sunny weather, contrasting with the service trams, but belonging to the same generation as the landaus — along the Golden Mile! *Steve Palmer*

Title page: A scene at North Pier in 1954, showing the 'Balloon' in the wartime green livery — which looks striking! 'Unloading only here' is the nearest sign, while the handsome building of Booths Grocery is in the background. *Roy Brook*

Below: THIS IS IT! No 1 is seen turning into the Pleasure Beach loop on 29 September 1960, ready to lead the procession. Here it is followed by No 2 of 1898, No 59 'Dreadnought' of 1902, and 'Standard' No 40 of 1924. *Fred Holland*

Introduction

When was the heyday of Blackpool trams? Well clearly in this book I will show some of the highlights in the long history of Blackpool Tramway during the past 50 years. Following World War 2, when Blackpool returned to the role of the hugely popular seaside resort, the trams were a vital part of the scene. The fleet, which included 116 streamliners from the 1930s, was under the leadership of General Manager Walter Luff and was to be further modernised before his retirement in 1954. He had succeeded in re-laying the Marton route and introducing fast streamlined trams, known as 'Marton Vambacs'. When the 25 'Coronation' trams had been introduced to the Promenade and Fleetwood route, he retired in a triumph of success! The 1960s climaxed early with the 75th Anniversary in 1960, with four restored vintage trams leading the procession, which culminated in a new trailer tram. These 10 trailer trams established a new generation for the fleet.

Following the fashion in other towns, with the closure of their tramway systems, Blackpool pruned its street routes while retaining the Promenade and Fleetwood Tramroad. Undoubtedly there were some memorable occasions in the 1960s, and the vintage trams were preserved by the National Tramway Museum at Crich. The new illuminated cars were introduced during that era, in memorable styles as seen today! The 1970s saw the introduction of home-built OMO cars, designed to save the increasing costs of operation, and the final withdrawal of the expensive 'Coronations'. The greatest heyday was reached in 1985, with the Centenary of the Promenade Tramway, and the appearance of vintage trams from a variety of British cities and Ireland. In this decade there were some triumphal epics, including the operation of Blackpool Boat trams in Glasgow and San Francisco, the introduction of new 'Centenary' trams here, and the return of the vintage 'Box-car' No 40. I sincerely hope that the future brings more heydays, with a new Tramway Age in Britain and the Centenary of the Blackpool & Fleetwood Tramroad here in 1998.

Steve Palmer
Fleetwood, December 1995

First published 1996

ISBN 0 7110 2459 6

Published by Ian Allan Publishing

an imprint of Ian Allan Ltd, Terminal House, Station Approach, Shepperton, Surrey TW17 8AS.
Printed by Ian Allan Printing Ltd, Coombelands House, Coombelands Lane, Addlestone, Weybridge, Surrey KT15 1HY.

Features of the 1950s

Above: The Pleasure Beach Casino in 1954, showing three trams in the green livery which was used in the war, but lasted many years afterwards. The leading 'Balloon' is one of the series 237–249, which were originally open-topped but enclosed in 1941–42, with their seating reduced to 84. Contrasting in style is the second 'Balloon' from series 250–263, with its cream shades above the windscreens and the trolley mounted on an arch, to allow the sunshine roofs to slide-open! Finally, the green railcoach — one of the 45 in series 200–224 and 264–283 — making the largest class of trams. All of these streamliners — including 'Boats' and 'Sun Saloons' — were built by English Electric in Preston during the 1930s, totalling 96. Additionally 20 railcars were built by Brush of Loughborough in 1937, thus creating a modern fleet of 116 trams before the war. *Roy Brook*

Above: In contrast to the prewar streamliners is this handsome 'Coronation' car of 1953, which has been introduced to the Promenade and Fleetwood route recently. The Inspector speaks to the seated driver in his comfortable cab as the 'Coronation' is about to turn on the loop. This postwar class of 25 trams rides smoothly and quickly for the 56 passengers seated comfortably. There is enough room on the large centre-platform for 20 passengers to be carried standing! In the saloons there is good viewing through the windows at all levels and through the roof! Being equipped with a UK version of the US PCC equipment, it was called VAMBAC: Variable Automatic Multinotch Braking & Acceleration Control. Thus the 'Coronations' — weighing 20 tons — could accelerate quickly and move at speed, 'to catch the seagulls,' the drivers said.
Roy Brook

Above: A busy scene at the Pleasure Beach on 24 May 1959, with two 'Pantograph' cars Nos 175 and 169 seen on a tour for the tram enthusiasts, and bound for Squires Gate via Starr Gate. They are showing '1' on their indicator blinds, since they only operate the North Station and Fleetwood route and never appear down the Promenade! This tour, travelling over the street routes in Blackpool, including Lytham Road, Station Road and Marton, was organised by Keith Terry of Leeds.

At this time, the Pleasure Beach featured the two Ferris wheels and the striking Casino of 1939 — just 20 years old! Here you can see the horse and landau, as well as the trams on the loop-line, all of which wait for their customers — at rush hour! *Richard Wiseman*

Above: The Welcome Arch at Starr Gate, with a view down South Promenade, which was opened by Lord Derby on 2 October 1926 to celebrate the Borough's Jubilee. Clearly this extended the Promenade tramway reservation beyond the Pleasure Beach to the terminal loop at Starr Gate. Here a street track was built to link with the Lytham St Anne's tramway in Clifton Drive, enabling trams to travel along the Promenade to their Gynn Square terminus, until it closed in 1937. One overhead wire can be seen, which enabled Blackpool Borough to use this track for its Circular Tour 1957–61. However, the Brush car No 303 is seen on the Promenade service, and thus will not turn left for Squires Gate. This tram is notable because it was equipped as the experimental 'Vambac' car in 1946, prior to the 12 'Marton Vambac' cars being created. Thus it is only used by its own Bispham Depot on the Promenade route, and never on North Station and Squires Gate routes. *Roy Brook*

Above: Squires Gate terminus in 1955, where the tram track turns the corner towards Squires Gate Lane Depot, but has been disused by trams since closure in 1937. However, it was retained during the war in case of dispersal of the Blackpool trams to the Lytham St Anne's Depot during air raids. The 'Balloons' are still in the wartime green livery and on the Lytham Road service, while the unusual 'Boat' No 227 is on a tour for the tram enthusiasts. Thus the 'Balloon' in the foreground is round the corner, having 'gone down for two' to allow the 'Boat' to reverse first and leave quickly on tour. It was unusual for a 'Boat' to be seen at Squires Gate until the Circular Tour started in 1957.

Roy Brook

7

Above: South Pier terminus of the Marton route, sees 'Vambac' No 14 having its trolley turned by the conductor, while the driver talks to two enthusiast passengers. Every third tram on the route travelled beyond Royal Oak during the summer season, running along Lytham Road and Station Road to this terminus. This was very useful for holidaymakers to travel from Marton to South Shore, or from here to Stanley Park. Buses also operate from here to Mereside, and the green roof of 1936–37 Leyland Titan TD4 with Burlingham body can be seen beyond the tram. At this terminus is the famous Pablos café with ice cream and also shops and boarding-houses. The buses on replacement service 26, introduced in 1962, today terminate here, and return to Marton using the Handy Buses. *Roy Brook*

Above: Outside Loxhams Rolls-Royce showrooms is seen a very smart 'Marton Vambac' car No 10 in May 1955, bound for Royal Oak. It has a few passengers after the morning rush hour, but the crew are watching the clock outside Marton Depot and waiting for time. In the 1950s these trams operated a three-minute service for the residents of Marton — a fine record! Above the tram can be seen the feeder-cable from the sub-station at the Depot, and in the foreground cobbles surrounding the depot approach track. The first of these modern trams, Nos 10–15, went into service on the Marton route in 1948–49, and by 1951 all 12, Nos 10–21, were fitted with Maley & Taunton bogies with resilient wheels and four Crompton Parkinson 45hp motors. These 12 cars and No 208 — the 'Vambac' railcoach — replaced the traditional double-deck 'Standards'.
Roy Brook

Above: Marton Depot in 1953 — home for the trams — showing the spacious interior of the 1901 building, with tiled walls and clean inspection pits. The depot is divided down the centre by the wartime air-raid shelter, into four tracks for the service cars and four for the summer 'Boat' cars, 'Standards' and illuminated cars. The depot was closed from 1939 until 1944, when it was used as a factory by the Vickers Aircraft Co. In May 1951 — for the 50th Anniversary — the elegant front of the depot was decorated with flags and bunting. In this scene, the single-deck trams are now in routine service while the three 'Standards' are used in peak periods as 'school specials' — complete with 78 seats! Along the wall on the left can be seen a red box for the fire hose, a display cabinet for the fleet numbers in location, and a desk with the signing-list for the drivers. The Marton Depot family was in good spirits, operating the exclusive route and independently sending 'Promenade specials' for the day.

Roy Brook

Above: A cheerful scene in Talbot Square, showing the two 'smiling' Marton trams on 31 May 1955, complete with the flares of their 1950s livery. On the left is 'Marton Vambac' No 11, and on the right is one of the familiar English Electric railcoaches, six of which were based at Marton Depot to help operate the service when needed. It is true that in addition to the 13 'Vambac' cars, a further six railcoaches should have been refitted, but the equipment and bogies were used as 'spares' for the 'Coronations'. Here their trolleys are crossed ready for reversal, and are fitted with swivel heads especially for the Marton route. There is an elegant shelter for passengers and a fine setting of buildings! Looking up Clifton Street towards the GPO, the next tram is waiting to reverse here. 'Hold tight — we're off!'

Roy Brook

Above: 'Boat' car No 230 is seen in Dickson Road on tour, strikingly pictured with the splendid Derby Baths in 1955, and their cream colour matching in the style of the 1930s. Opened in 1939 and named after Lord Derby, these baths had a pool of Olympic size, a tier of diving boards, a sunbathing terrace and rows of tiered seats for the spectators. Clearly the tram stops on the Promenade and Dickson Road at Warley Road were always named 'Derby Baths' for the benefit of the passengers.

Children and adults — with rolls of towels and swimming costumes — were always seen travelling there by tram. On Saturdays, the children when leaving the baths would travel by Dickson Road trams to the Odeon Club where — for only 6d — you had a full morning's entertainment. However, in this scene the passengers are tram enthusiasts and you might recognise some of them? Today there are no trams here — and no Derby Baths! *Roy Brook*

Above: Gynn Square in 1954 with 'Pantograph' No 173 destined for North Station and correctly showing service '1' in its saloon indicator box. Named after their original pantographs in 1928, Nos 167–176 were officially called 'Pullmans', and were built by Dick Kerr Works at Preston. They were the first municipal trams on this route, following the take-over of the Blackpool & Fleetwood Tramroad Co in 1920, and were the first trams to be fitted with the now-familiar trolley tower. They were well received by the public in the 1920s because they had comfortable moquette on the 48 seats — apart from two on each platform. However, they had high steps on to the tram, and were thought of as old-fashioned in the 1930s when compared with the new 'Streamliners'. No 173 is in the postwar livery from 1945 to 1961 (after which they were withdrawn). However, three can be seen in Blackpool today in disguise as illuminated cars but No 173 was scrapped, and restored No 167 is at the National Tramway Museum.

Roy Brook

13

Above: A scene on the track fan of Bispham Depot — July 1958 — showing the new Engineering car No 3, and looking towards Red Bank Road. This was originally 'Standard' No 143, rebuilt for maintenance of the overhead. It has a raised platform on the top deck and is powered by a TD4 Leyland bus engine, driving a generator in the lower saloon. This meant that in the event of power failure, No 3 could proceed without the trolley poles — mounted at each end — and feed self-generated power into the overhead. It is true that No 3 is still seen here in the 'Standard' livery, but the windows of the lower saloon are slatted to give ventilation. This car was based at Bispham Depot for good access to the northern Tramroad. By October 1961, the top deck saloons were removed to provide an open platform for inspection and access to the overhead. Today it may be restored as 'Standard' No 143 by Blackpool Transport Services, which will be popular with its seasonal tourists — for its open balconies!
Roy Brook

Above: In 1955 a railcoach is seen passing through Cleveleys Square, a location which is complete with reserved track through the roundabout. This was always an attractive centre, with gardens and the official Thornton Cleveleys UDC coat of arms. While today there is no roundabout, most of the buildings are intact — including the National Westminster Bank, Citizens Advice Bureau and the green tram shelters. Notice the wooden slats to keep pedestrians and traffic from the reserved tram track, which makes it exclusive for the trams! The handsome livery of the railcoach is seen in the 1950s, but the original beading shows the prewar style! *Roy Brook*

Above: At Thornton Gate — 7 April 1957 — is 'Pantograph' No 174, newly repainted, during a tram tour bound for Ash Street. The hut of the duty point-boy can be seen on the right, used when the points were regularly needed by service cars and until 1949 by the train of wagons. The sidings here were built in 1927 and were used by the electric locomotive pulling wagons from the railway at Fleetwood to deliver coal. Local coal merchants collected it here for delivery locally — a fine achievement of the Blackpool-owned Tramroad! Everything changes, and 'Pantograph' No 174 became the trailer for the illuminated Western Train in 1962; it may return to its striking guise for the Centenary in 1998.
Richard Wiseman

Above: Here is Fleetwood Copse Road Depot, used by the Permanent Way Department, with 'Pantograph' No 167 and the electric locomotive of 1927 with its track-spraying trailer — formerly toastrack No 161. Both are able to tow the rail-carrying bogies to re-laying locations, seen here. The depot was built in 1897 for the Blackpool & Fleetwood Tramroad Co, and had a link with the Lancashire & Yorkshire Railway, enabling railway wagons to be shunted on to the Tramroad. In 1927 this was developed for the delivery of coal to Thornton Gate by a train of wagons led by the electric locomotive. It is true that local children used to collect fallen pieces of coal off the tram track for their own home fires. Today the depot building is the sole survivor of the Tramroad Co, complete with engraved headstones, and used by a car seller. The two trams are now used at the National Tramway Museum: No 167 carrying passengers and the loco for shunting trams. *Roy Brook*

17

Above: At St Peter's parish church in Lord Street, where the railcoach stops for passengers. One day in 1955, a little boy stands watching the passengers boarding the tram, but there is little traffic to pose a risk. The *Highway Code* does state that traffic must stop to allow passengers to step into the road to board trams. The striking red hoop on the opposite pole shows the 'Cars Stop By Request' tram stop — from a distance. In Albert Square is the office of the *Evening Gazette* and the *Fleetwood Chronicle*, and today all the buildings are intact — including *'J. S. Walker & Sons'* for menswear. In 1996 trams are still in service — and busy on market days! *Roy Brook*

Above: Fleetwood Ferry terminus with 'Standard' No 40 and 'Coronation' No 325 pictured on 24 May 1959, during a tour for enthusiasts. This was the first visit of a 'Standard' car to Fleetwood, following the introduction of double-deckers to this route in 1958. At this terminal loop, which was constructed in 1925, it is possible to see the vintage North Euston Hotel, designed by Decimus Burton in 1841, and the lifeboat house. The channel of the River Wyre can be seen with a ship in the distance, and the scenery of Morecambe Bay. The sailing of the Isle of Man Steam Packet Co ships to Douglas commenced in 1842, and reached their 150th year in 1992. This was marked by the sailing of a fully-dressed *Lady of Mann*, still in service today. Passengers have been able to visit here from Douglas using a new Seacat, and board the tram to Blackpool!

Roy Brook

The 75th Anniversary — 1960

Above: A historic scene on 9 July 1960, during the first tour by the Tramway Museum Society with 1898 'Crossbench' car No 2 and 1902 'Dreadnought' No 59, which pose together in Pharos Street by the lighthouse. These trams had been restored for the 75th Anniversary, fortunately having survived after withdrawal: No 2 as works car 127 at Copse Road Depot and 'Dreadnought' No 59 stored there.

The whole class of 'Dreadnoughts' was broken up after its withdrawal in 1934, but a phone call by Manager Walter Luff gave clear instructions to save the last one — No 59. This was in response to correspondence in the *Evening Gazette* advocating the preservation of at least one of this unique type. The class of 20 'Dreadnoughts' was made unique by Blackpool's purchase of the patent design by Mr Shrewsbury of Camwell in 1897. They had end-loading by broad steps and had twin staircases surrounding the driver at each end, allowing simultaneous entrance and exit by the passengers. On this tour the riders could enjoy the sea-breezes in two ways! *Roy Brook*

Above: On the same day — after the TMS tour — the 'Dreadnought' seen in its original municipal livery of red and ivory contrasts with the other green and cream trams at the Pleasure Beach loop. The 'Standards' seen here were built by Blackpool Transport in the 1920s: No 41 of 1925 is seen passing No 48 of 1928, which is followed by an illuminated 'Standard' and 'Balcony' No 40 of 1926. By 1960 eight of these 'Standards' were used as 'specials' on the Promenade, fully-enclosed apart from 'Balcony' No 40. It was not unique by then because 'Balcony' No 144 went to the Seashore Trolley Museum, Maine, USA in 1955, and operated there. Today 'Standards' Nos 40 and 49 are to be seen at the National Tramway Museum in Derbyshire, while No 159 operated at the East Anglia Transport Museum, Carlton Colville. Blackpool does still have a remaining 'Standard' No 143 — converted to an Engineering car — which may be restored for the Centenary in 1998. *Roy Brook*

Above: On 29 September 1960, a procession of 11 trams started from the Pleasure Beach, where they assembled from three depots, and loaded at North Pier as seen here. Manager Joe Franklin can be seen with his clipboard surveying the leaders of the commemorative procession, before starting them off for Little Bispham. Members of the public were all carried free of charge, and boarded the trams of their choice — with the vintage ones first! However, they were not allowed to sit on the open top of the 1885 No 1, which was thought to be dangerous for them. Originally this tram drew its power from the conduit between the running rails, and was converted to trolley-collection in 1898. In reality it was No 4, built by the Lancaster Railway & Carriage Co in 1885, and thus was renumbered No 4 for the Centenary in 1985. On that second eventful occasion it was deprived of its trolley and powered by batteries to re-create the 1885 conduit system. *Fred Holland*

Above: THIS IS IT! At Little Bispham the first three trams pose for the photographers, with the passengers smiling and driver Gilly Potter holding the controls — wearing gloves. There were 11 trams in the procession, showing the history of the tramway from 1885 until 1960, with a twin-set's brand new trailer No T3 at the end. This was intended to prove that Blackpool had 'Progress' with streamliners of the 1930s and 'Coronation' No 321 of the 1950s. Thus the future seemed secure! *Fred Holland*

Left: The open-top 'Dreadnought' became popular from 1960 to 1965, when it departed to the National Tramway Museum. Here No 59 is seen at the Foxhall, travelling on the Promenade Circular amidst thousands of people strolling along the Promenade. People wore more trendy clothing in the early sixties but the woman seen in the Waller & Hartley Milady advert is in full evening dress! The 'Dreadnought' is situated nicely between the Central Pier of 1868 and the Tower of 1894 — thus making a vintage trio from Blackpool. However, 59 does advertise 'Milk for Stamina' and the Milk Race by bike in June 1963. *Steve Palmer*

Right: On Monday 16 September 1963, vintage crossbench car No 2 is seen returning from storage in Copse Road depot, Fleetwood. Clearly it is 'Reserved' while passing the Imperial Hotel, but travels the Coastal Tramway for the last time. It departed for the National Tramway Museum on 29 September 1963 and became the first tram to carry passengers there in 1964. No 2 still operates today, and it is hoped that it will return here to celebrate the Blackpool & Fleetwood Tramroad Centenary on 1 July 1998. *Steve Palmer*

Sights of the Sixties

Above: Ferry to Knott End on Sea' in June 1964, as 'Progress Twin Car' Nos 278-T8 waits on the siding for passengers. The programme of introducing Twin-cars began with two rebuilt railcoaches Nos 276 and 275 in April 1958, and was completed in 1962 with rebuilding 10 railcoaches and buying 10 new trailers. These were built by MCW of Birmingham, with Maley & Taunton 5ft 6in wheelbase bogies, and were of handsome appearance resembling the 1953 'Coronations'. Whilst it had been the

intention for them to operate a limited-stop service, this caused difficulties for the confused passengers. In 1961 Nos 281-T1 were permanently coupled with a driver's cab fitted at the reverse end of the trailer. By 1970 seven sets were completed, but sadly the work was not completed and Nos 278–280 were permanently separated from their trailers. The three trailers Nos T8-T10 were finally scrapped, having been variously loaned for trials with GEC and West Yorkshire Transport Museum in Bradford. The existing seven twin-cars with 114 seats are valuable today, during the busy periods on Fleetwood market days and during the Illuminations.
Roy Brook

Above: The famous 'Dreadnought' is seen at Fleetwood Ash Street in 1965, on its last tour for TMS members before it left for Crich Museum on 18 March. The stylish shelter here was built after the take-over by Blackpool Borough in 1920, and follows a similar style to those on the Marton route. The weather vane and the clock tower surmounted waiting rooms, inspectors' office and facilities for the public. Subsequently it was demolished when traffic lights were installed, and the tram stop moved to the end of the reservation. Today we have an improved scene, with Fisherman's Walk complete with clock tower, gardens and sea anchors. The trams have their own traffic lights, which gives them precedence over cars and buses. *Steve Palmer*

Above: On 19 September 1963, 'Pantograph' No 170 — showing 'Permanent Way' on its indicator — approaches a new road crossing being made for Larkholme Avenue. Still in the fleet livery, No 170 took the place of No 167 when the latter left for Crich in December 1962, and is seen here returning from delivering new rail to trackworks near the Ferry. While building is taking place here, it is possible to see the engine sheds in the background, where the Preston & Wyre Railway first arrived in 1840. Looking at the tram track, it is clear to see the check-rails added in 1958, when double-deckers were used on the Fleetwood route for the first time. This was dictated by the Transport Ministry, but subsequently was discontinued as not necessary. When riding by tram today, look out for the site of the engine sheds — now occupied by the famous factory of Fisherman's Friend.

Steve Palmer

Left: Broadwater pictured in 1960, depicting the new Engineering car No 3 at the road crossing of the A585 into Fleetwood. The passengers are waiting for a tram coming, but sadly No 3 will not give them a ride! Approaching on service 14 is one of the hundred famous Leyland PD2/5 buses of 1949–51, with bodies built by Burlinghams of Blackpool. This is a busy community with a housing estate, the Fleetwood Cricket Club and Broadwater Post Office. Traffic makes this crossing busy, as evidenced by the Foden truck, and the drivers have to give way to trams crossing. There is a crossover here, where local trams reverse on the local Broadwater & Ferry service on market days. Today no trams reverse here, and the residents have the choice of taking trams or buses or going by bike! *Steve Palmer*

Above: One of the distinctive 'Coronation' cars seen in service, bound for Starr Gate and passing Rossall School in August 1964. This section of the Tramroad is still in a rural setting with two farms and the playing fields of the 1844 public school. It is interesting that Rossall School is on the site of Rossall Hall, home of Sir Peter Hesketh-Fleetwood, who inherited the coastline in 1824 and commenced the development of Fleetwood. In this view can be seen the sea-wall, the school open-air baths, the school chapel and the clock tower amongst the many school buildings. Of course pupils from the school use the trams when they are allowed out at weekends and at the end of the school-day. Recently — in 1994 — HM The Queen and HRH The Duke of Edinburgh visited the school, and tramway passengers got a grandstand view. *Steve Palmer*

REDUCE
SPEED HERE
TO
4 MILES PER HOUR

ROSSALL BEACH

NORTH STATION
BLACKPOOL

Above: Brush car 300 at Rossall Beach stop in August 1963, showing the neat style of a Tramroad stop: with the title board, red hoops on the pole with 'Cars Stop by Request' sign, and the black and amber hoops. This was a new indication of the limited stops for the trailer trams here, and so the paved platform was lengthened. The 'Reduce Speed Here' notice for drivers is appropriate, for the farm's drive crossing, while passengers standing by the fence should beware of the cows, bulls or sometimes geese! Across the fields can be seen Fleetwood power station opened in the 1950s but subsequently demolished. Clearly the service tram is destined for 'North Station Blackpool', and owing to the new single-indicator box cannot show the traditional service number '1'. *Steve Palmer*

Right: Thornton Gate siding on 26 August 1963, showing the decapitated Engineering car No 3 leaving — having delivered railcoach No 202 from Bispham Depot — for scrapping. While this was the mineral siding from 1927 until 1949, it became the centre for the Permanent Way Department in 1963, following the closure of the Copse Road Depot. A stock of rail can be seen, with a crane able to lift the rails on to the bogie-trailers for transportation along the Tramroad. Works cars can be seen at this siding when collecting new rail and returning old rail, to this day. During controversy about the future of the Blackpool & Fleetwood Tramroad in the 1970s — and again in 1995 — Blackpool sought the retention of the sidings, even if the tramway was curtailed at Cleveleys. However, the continued rewiring north of Thornton Gate will depend upon the financial contribution of Wyre Borough Council. *Steve Palmer*

Left: At Whitsuntide 1964, a busy scene at Norbreck station outside the Hydro — now known as Norbreck Castle Hotel — with many 'Coronation' cars. Nos 308 and 304 are in the traditional cream livery, while No 310 is subdued in half green and cream livery with an orange tower. During the winter of 1963–4, No 310 had been fitted with 64 bus seats, while No 323 in this livery had its 'Vambac' equipment removed and replaced by a conventional EE Z6 controller. This began a process of cutting operational costs of the 'Coronations', and thus reduced their performance. While the OAPs snooze on the bench outside the station building, a family admire the attractive 'Coronation' trams on the tramway.
Steve Palmer

Above: Bispham Top is seen, with Brush car No 291 emerging from Red Bank Road and its native Bispham Depot on 14 August 1963. The scene looks very familiar today with the bank and shops in Red Bank Road — but without the trams travelling up and down to Bispham Depot, which has been demolished to allow Sainsbury's supermarket to be built on the site. Of course this location dates back to the foundation of the Tramroad Co in 1898, and was the site of the depot, the workshops, power station and the large family house, 'Pooldhooie', for the Manager John Cameron. Today the large house is still there, and now the Conservative Club, together with the bowling green. The Bispham Hotel, next to the former depot yard, appropriately shows a tram on its sign outside, and the trams can be seen passing on the Promenade.
Steve Palmer

Above: 'Balloon' No 237 is showing 'North Station Blackpool' on its indicators while standing at the end of the line outside the Odeon on 26 October 1963. It shows a unique new livery at the time, but sadly this is the penultimate day of the route. The location of the original terminus outside North station was shortened at Easter 1961, with the provision of a trolley reverser. This was created to relieve conductors from turning the trolleys in the busy traffic, and copies the Royal Oak terminus elsewhere. Traffic could now pass the reversing trams — with their trolleys swinging out at right-angles to the tram — in complete safety. However, it lasted only until 27 October 1963, when buses replaced the trams on route 25A to Cleveleys. While service 1 was heavily used by residents in the peak hours, during the day the holidaymakers came here to board trams for the Fleetwood Market. Thus it became necessary to send the 94-seat 'Balloons' — but never the 'Coronations' or the Twincars. The scene along Dickson Road is very similar today, but without the trams to Fleetwood — which should have been retained! *Steve Palmer*

33

Above: Squires Gate terminus at the Airport, pictured with a railcoach reversing over the crossover — returning to the town centre and North Shore. The Hillman Minx saloon is turning into Squires Gate Lane where the tram track and overhead, belonging to Lytham St Annes, is still in place. The north track was used by the Circular Tour from 1957 until 1961, when this route closed. On 29 October railcoach No 268 left Squires Gate for Manchester Square for the last time, and buses took its place on route 12 the next day. This was a very busy route with a five-minute service, with alternate trams bound for Cabin and Bispham. Local residents used it from the town centre, where there were separate shelters from the Promenade trams. Holidaymakers sometimes used them, following instructions 'Watsons Road for the Pleasure Beach' on the shelters — and unfortunately ended up with a long walk! *Steve Palmer*

Right: Travelling along Lytham Road from Squires Gate, railcoach No 203 is drawing away from the shelter and is about to pass the Dunes Hotel on 29 October 1961 — the last day. This tram is bound for Bispham, one of seven provided by Bispham Depot which gave a 10min service, carrying duty cards 51–57. The traction poles on Lytham Road are attractive with their delicate street lights in pairs of bulbs with reflectors. The tram stops are clearly shown with the red hoops together with the circular 'Polo' signs. Being a residential area, the houses are positioned distinctively with large gardens and trees. The railcoach carries the Illuminations lights upon its trolley tower and is painted with the cream front adopted in 1958.
Fred Holland

Above: Station Road, South Shore, seen on the last day of the seasonal extension of the Marton route — 29 October 1961 — with railcoach No 219 leaving the terminus. It is on the crossover with its trolley at an angle, allowed by its swivel-head! By this time there is nobody going to the cafeteria for fish and chips at 1s 9d, but a handsome Vauxhall is in the foreground. This line, linking Lytham Road with the Promenade at South Pier, was built as a final extension to the conduit system in 1895 and converted to overhead three years later. At the end of the street can be seen the original entrance to South Station, now moved to Waterloo Road. That was the original terminus of the Lytham St Annes gas trams in 1896, and electric trams to town thereafter. Today Station Road looks similar, albeit without the trams.

Fred Holland

Right: At Royal Oak junction, 'Marton Vambac' No 15 turns into Waterloo Road, served by a point-boy on duty there, while the railcoach behind waits to proceed directly to the town centre along Lytham Road. This is the last day of the Lytham Road route on 29 October 1961, after which the Marton cars terminated here for 12 months. The junction had been re-laid during the winter of 1958, during which period the buses had taken over from trams temporarily. However, this led to the Council coming to the conclusion to convert the route, on the grounds of cost. *Fred Holland*

Left: 'Standard' No 40 is pictured at Royal Oak, turning right into Lytham Road during a farewell tour of this route on 29 October 1961. This striking view, with the shining track in front of the Royal Oak Hotel, provides a nostalgic view for everyone. *Fred Holland*

Above: The scene shows Talbot Square in July 1962, as the driver swings the trolley of 'Marton Vambac' No 13 prior to its journey to Royal Oak, providing a four-minute service. Here we are looking towards the North Pier, seeing crowds of people and Bernard Delfont's 'Show of Stars' advertised. This is a busy scene on the traffic island, with the strolling people and the elegant stone shelter with adjacent telephone booth. Here is the Bundy time-clock, where each conductor registers his tram's departure time on his waybill. Until 1936 the trams for Layton — via Talbot Road — used to load at the island, and by this time south-bound buses loaded here. Today traffic surrounds the island together with a taxi rank, and the buses are relegated to the kerb at each side of the Square, but no trams and shelter.
Steve Palmer

Right: An elevated view of Clifton Street — taken from the roof of the present Blackpool Publicity Office — shows modernised railcoach No 208 heading towards the General Post Office in Abingdon Street. No 208, like the 'Marton Vambac' trams, was able to accelerate rapidly in Clifton Street, leaving cars and buses standing. This demonstrated the performance of modern trams — like the American PCC cars. In 1962 — the last summer season with service trams here — they well suit the scene with commercial buildings and shops. The tram tracks leave enough room for cars to park at each side of the street, but they discipline traffic following trams into lines. Today the scene is similar — but without the trams.
Steve Palmer

Above: A view of Church Street from the curve into Abingdon Street, as traditional Marton 'Standard' No 40 approaches by a final tour on 28 October 1962. While a man races the trams to the corner, the front of the Opera House & Winter Gardens provides a traditional setting, together with Vernon Humpage shoe shop. Looking down Church Street can be seen the white dome of the Regent Cinema dominated by the rebuilding of the Hippodrome Theatre into the ABC Theatre and Cinema; St John's parish church of 1829 is on the left, with the bus stop in front of its garden, clear of the tram tracks. On the following day, the buses will have it all to themselves. Of course the 'Standards' like No 40 exclusively operated this route until replaced by the 'Marton Vambacs' in the early 1950s. *Fred Holland*

Above: On Whitegate Drive the two trams Nos 11 and 17 pass at Beechfield Avenue where there is a tram stop. Passengers wait at the roadside until the tram stops, when they walk out to board with the traffic halted by the conductor's raised arm. In the *Highway Code* traffic is supposed to overtake trams on the inside and beware of the passengers. By 1962 undoubtedly traffic in Whitegate Drive was so busy that the trams were replaced by buses at the end of the season. However, residents always enjoyed and appreciated the trams because they had the finest regular four-minute service in Blackpool. Today the Handy Buses operate the same route for Blackpool Transport, but undoubtedly the Marton trams were famous in their day. This was the last street tram route in the UK, after the closure of Glasgow city trams in September 1962.
Steve Palmer

Left: Marton Depot with a service tram waiting at the stop — complete with shelter — showing the elegant appearance with municipal arms over the doors. The depot office can be seen on the left, where the duty inspector was in charge of the office and traffic money could be paid in by the conductors. The service car stands on the main line, and there is a siding from which the depot tracks curve. Here crews used to change over at the end of their shift and were relieved for a break in the staff canteen. Open doors show the four service tracks, while the closed doors indicate the storage part of the depot. On the newsagents is an eye-catching poster for Ovaltine, while the Saddle Inn of 1776 stands at the corner of Preston Old Road. Today these are both present, while the depot site is occupied by a BP service station. *Steve Palmer*

Above: Royal Oak terminus of the Marton route on 28 October 1962, with 'Standard' No 48 present. On this last day of operation there were many tours by trams for enthusiasts who were marking the departure of the final street tramway in Britain. This tram is now in the Glenwood Trolley Park, Oregon, USA, where it has been repainted and is operated. No 48 was built in 1928 with the old top-cover from a 1902 Motherwell, hence the short upper saloon visible here (and on No 49 at Crich today). Today there are no trams at Royal Oak, but the public house is still there, while the Palladium Cinema — here showing *Ben Hur* — now offers bingo.
Steve Palmer

Above: On the evening of 28 October 1962, the final service journeys of 'Marton Vambacs' Nos 11 and 13 were replaced by 'Standards' Nos 40 and 48, Talbot Square and Royal Oak respectively. They were filled by tram enthusiasts; whilst it was a quiet departure from Royal Oak and a speedy journey along Waterloo Road, it was a formal occasion at Talbot Square. 'Standard' No 40 was joined by the two illuminated 'Standards' Nos 158 and 159 which travelled in convoy through the town centre. A large crowd of local residents gathered outside Marton Depot to witness the departure of their trams. Here is a dramatic scene as 'Standard' No 159 illuminates the scene before it enters the depot and unloads its official passengers from the Town Council. Two buses are waiting on the forecourt to transport the guests back to a party at the Transport Offices. When the depot doors were shut and the buses departed down Whitegate Drive, a sad observer commented: 'MARTON has now become NOTRAM!'
Fred Holland

a scene in Church Street on 31 May 1963, when the illuminated
...ved with the Mayor, outside the new ABC Cinema and Theatre.
...s the new show, starring Cliff Richard and the Shadows, and the
...itness the opening ceremony. All this was very exciting, but
...amway enthusiasts, as a scheduled tram appeared for the first time
...nce the route closed in 1962. It is true that the tramway overhead

was retained to the theatre, so that the ABC-sponsored Western Train could take part
in their special occasion! Once the ceremony was over the Mayor entered to see
Holiday Carnival and the tram reversed down Church Street to Talbot Square,
becoming the last tram in the town centre. Subsequently the overhead was
dismantled and the track covered over, and today there are no trams, the ABC is the
MGM and Cliff Richard has been knighted in 1995! *Fred Holland*

Above: 12 January 1963 — a frosty scene on the Pleasure Beach loop with the two No 40s on the final tour before they leave for the National Tramway Museum. What is the problem? All the enthusiasts are gathered round 'Standard' No 40 because it is stuck on the curve, its wheels spinning in the thick frost. the driver did get it moving with applications of sand to the wheels — and a push from the enthusiasts.

On that day the two trams journeyed along the Promenade to Little Bispham and back to the Pleasure Beach, 'Box' No 40 of 1914 representing the Tramroad Co and 'Standard' No 40 of 1926 the Borough of Blackpool. In contrasting liveries and design, the two cars are not exactly twins and from different families.
Roy Brook

Right: On the following day there was an excursion to Fleetwood with ex-conduit No 1 and 'Box' No 40. It was a very chilly ride on the open-top deck, when the passengers' hair turned white and the driver's glasses frosted up. Here at Rossall it is a wintry scene, as No 1 stands on the points of the wartime siding, and during the tour it was amazing that ice could be seen floating on the sea! During the afternoon there was a tour to North Station with 'Dreadnought' No 59 and B&F 'Crossbench' No 2, and finally with 'Marton Vambac' No 11 which had been rescued from Marton Depot. Due to the perception of the tour organiser — Keith Terry — No 11 has been preserved and can be seen at East Anglia Transport Museum today. Why were these historic trams leaving Blackpool in 1963, when they had been restored for the 75th Anniversary in 1960? Well Blackpool followed the fashion in Leeds, Sheffield and Glasgow in replacing the street routes by buses. Consequently the fleet was contracting to serve the Promenade and Fleetwood route, and only one depot was to be retained. Thus there was no room — and the restored trams were transferred to museums.
Steve Palmer

Above: A striking view of Derby Baths on 25 March 1964, as English Electric railcoach No 268 — bound for Fleetwood — passes Grinder car No 2. Of course this was the winter season when trams operated only between Fleetwood and Cleveleys, and buses operated route 25 along the Promenade. The passengers were warned on the tram-stop signs that buses will stop on the road opposite, but there will be one tram each day for Fleetwood at 4pm. However, there was so much objection by Fleetwood and Cleveleys councils, that a passenger ballot was held at Cleveleys. It was found that the majority wanted to return to having a through tram service for the whole of the year. At Easter 1964, the trams returned to a Starr Gate and Fleetwood service, and in preparation the two Grinder cars cleaned the Promenade track. Undoubtedly the Derby Baths — sadly demolished in 1990 — was one of the sights of the Promenade and today there is an empty site next to the Pembroke Hotel.
Steve Palmer

Above: A delightful evening scene on the Promenade in 1964, as 'Standard' No 160 leaves the shelter for the Pleasure Beach, and some passengers. Approaching is a Twin-car bound for Little Bispham, looking very clean in its all-cream livery with green lining, while a 'Coronation' follows. A bus on route 12 for Squires Gate will remind us of the departed trams in 1961. The new Lewis's store with its rectangular white-tiled profile dominates the scene over the Tower building. This was built on the site of the famous Palace Building with theatre, cinema and ballroom, which closed and was demolished in 1962. Today Lewis's has closed and the building has been restyled in the red-brick appearance of the Tower, housing Mecca Bingo, Woolworth's and Harry Ramsden's Chip Restaurant. *Steve Palmer*

Illuminated Trams

Above: Illuminated trams Progress and the Lifeboat are seen outside the North Pier in 1955, with their lights reflected in the wet Promenade. In the 1950s, the illuminated trams toured the Illuminations as a spectacular contribution to the scene, without passengers. However, the Lifeboat of 1926 did carry special parties of guests — including the employees' children. Being constructed on the frame of Marton 'Box-car' No 40, it had a four-wheel truck which gave a bouncing trip over the sleeper-track. Progress originated as the Bandwagon in 1937, representing the concept of a tram for 2037, but was used during the war to advertise slogans in daylight. For the 1949 Illuminations — the first after the war — it was rebuilt as the Progress car, representing a double-decker with silhouette passengers in the windows, and broadcasting a musical sound. 1958 became the final year for the Progress car, since one side depicted a tableau of the sailing ship *Mayflower.* While this looked very picturesque, it weakened the structure and was withdrawn and stripped down to reveal the original Tramroad car No 141. *Sic transit gloria!*
Roy Brook

Above: When the Illuminations were popularly revived in 1925, the Gondola was created upon the frame of the 1901 four-wheeled Marton 'Box-car' No 28. With its attractive form of elevated bows and the elegant pagoda surmounted by an illuminated lantern, the Gondola became unique on Blackpool Promenade. Looking at this portrait in the depot, it is possible to identify the wooden planks beneath the painted canvas of the hull, and the railings which indicated the driver's bridge. Passengers were not normally carried on the Gondola apart from special occasions, such as when the personality who had performed the Switch-on ceremony was taken for a tour along the Promenade. In the 1960s a special entrance was created in the side to admit paying passengers, and they experienced pitching and rolling over the sleeper-track — just like a maritime voyage! Sadly, after a collision with another tram in 1962, the Gondola was withdrawn — and scuttled! There are many happy memories of this beautiful tram.
Steve Palmer collection

Left: In 1959 the *Blackpool Belle* replaced the Progress car, and became the first of a new generation. It carried 32 passengers. Seen here at North Pier while loading passengers for a tour, its handsome appearance as an American paddle-steamer is shown by the illuminated paddle-wheels. While the passengers sit facing out, the coloured compartments on the top-deck contain the musical equipment to accompany the voyage. The waves along the bows are illuminated by flickering lights, while the funnel conceals the trolley stanchion. Of course the *Blackpool Belle* was constructed on a wooden frame upon the last surviving 'Toastrack', No 163, which was driven from Copse Road Depot to the works in the spring of 1959. Since 1982 the *Belle* has transferred to Oregon USA, where it sails in the Trolley museum. *Steve Palmer*

Right: Blackpool Promenade in October 1961 — and, look out, here comes an illuminated rocket *Tramnik One*! It commemorated the first space flight of the Soviet earth satellite Sputnik. The angled fuselage at 20° was constructed upon 'Pantograph' No 168, with the driver's cab underneath. The conductor has to communicate with the driver by a buzzer, and the 46 passengers are seated in the fuselage covered with bulbs. It can be reversed by being driven from the rear entrance through the rocket-exhaust. *Fred Holland*

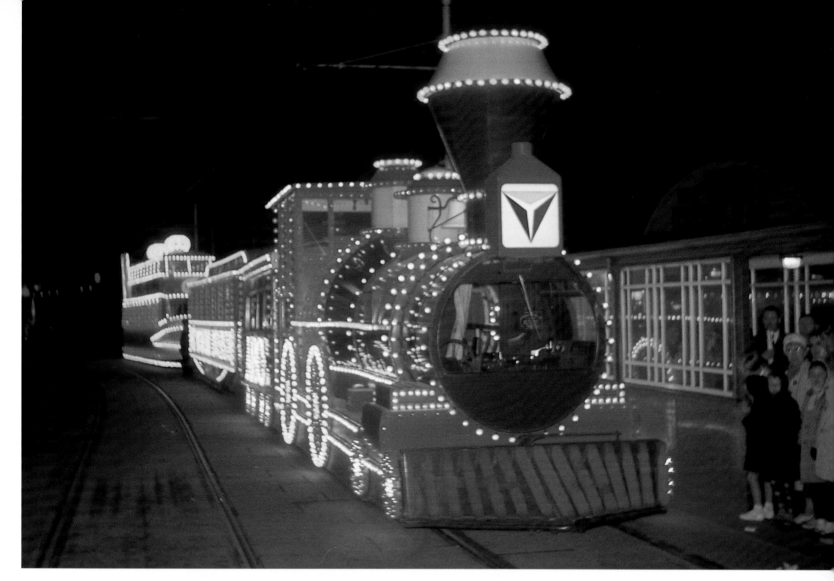

Above: The Western Train of 1962 followed the practice of the Twin-cars at the time, using the towing equipment, and was built from railcoach No 209 and 'Pantograph' No 174. It was rumoured that the wife of Manager Joe Franklin created the idea after watching a Western film depicting a vintage locomotive in the USA. While it has been used in 1995, it is hoped that the carriage may be restored to its true identity as 'Pantograph' car No 174 for the Tramroad Centenary in 1998. Original features include smoke from the funnel and an illuminated cow-catcher at the front, while the brass bell can be rung by the driver from his cab — by rope. The passengers on the locomotive sit within the tender, while those in the carriage have a better view. Behind is the Hovertram of 1963, built upon railcoach No 222, with the large capacity of 99 passengers uniquely low-bridge style upstairs. The engines are on the roof, and it has a low side-aisle with four cross bench padded seats. *Steve Palmer*

53

Look Out — Trams About

Above: A very pleasant 1973 evening scene at North Pier, with No 1 — the first of the OMO trams introduced into service in the autumn of 1972. The OMO trams were designed by Chief Engineer Alan Williams, extending the bodies of prewar railcoaches to 49ft, with front entrances. This enabled drivers to collect fares and drive the tram; hence operating costs could be saved, especially in winter. In the 1970s costs became a threat to the future of the Blackpool & Fleetwood Tramroad, with the reduction in passengers and increase in the expense of two-crew service trams. Manager Joe Franklin was determined to save the coastal tramway, having lost the town street tramway in the 1960s, thus he introduced the home-built new generation of service trams. The livery — known as 'plum and custard' — distinguished them as pay-as-you-enter trams for the passengers. Thus Blackpool Transport was able to bid for a grant from the Department of Transport towards the cost of the OMOs, unique in Britain amongst a generation of OMO buses! *Roy Brook*

Above: A striking view of OMO No 3 at Bispham in October 1972, during the training of drivers on the new trams. Of course the drivers had to learn about the ticket machine and collecting fares with their left hand, while operating the controller with their right hand. This was a new experience for tram drivers, who had always driven by left hand, and being alone in their cab did not meet passengers. Looking at No 3's design, the tapering entrance makes the tram look sharpened down to a single windscreen. The small dash panel is decorated by the coat of arms with the garter scroll. The passengers, who had to get used to ringing the bell for the next stop, and leaving at the centre door, were observed by the driver through the wing mirror. It really was 'Progress' by Blackpool Borough! *Ian McLoughlin*

Left: Tower in 1972 — passengers board the large rebuilt railcoach with the distinctive tapered end and increased capacity to 56 seats. This was railcoach No 271 (later No 618) — one of only 13 remaining — as a possible alternative to the large 'Coronations', which were expensive to operate. However, the next move — with the remaining railcoaches — was to use this design, and front entrance, for the OMOs. No 618 remained running in this form until finally becoming OMO No 13 in June 1976. It will be heading for Fleetwood in service, but the guard has not turned the nearest indicator, thus naming the location. Notice the long trolley — like that on the 'Coronation' — to be reached for turning by the trolley pole. *Roy Brook*

Right: At Fleetwood Ferry in July 1975 is seen Tigeriffic Brush car No 622, the first single-decker in all-over advertising livery, for Blackpool Zoo Park. It is true that this style — with tiger's face on each end and tigers leaping from the side doors — was very attractive and eye-catching. Many advertising liveries have followed to this day; some are memorable and some are best forgotten! *Steve Palmer*

Above: Seen passing through Cleveleys Square in July 1975 is 'Balloon' 707, the first to be in all-over advertising livery. The colourful front design — without words — caused the tram to be known as the Smarties car, and not Empire Pools! It is interesting to realise that No 707 has carried all-over advertising for 20 years, but is presently fitted with a new design at the front — which will once again change the scene!
Steve Palmer

Above: A view from the new pedestrian bridge across the tramway and the carriageway in June 1976, giving us a new perspective of the Promenade. OMO No 9 in plum and custard livery is outshone by Smartie No 707 next to it, since the OMO livery did not stand up to the weather. Looking at the three Promenade buildings, the Tower Wonderland of the World now seems to be sandwiched between the 1937 Woolworth's building and the 1964 Lewis's store, which has many flags to catch the eye. The pedestrian bridge was constructed from the new Palace Nightclub, on the site of the memorable Palatine Hotel, but was criticised for its obstruction of the scene. As it is not used very much today, it may not have been necessary after all. *Steve Palmer*

Right: Look out — trams about! in June 1975, with OMOs Nos 3 and 11 in two different liveries at Manchester Square. In this year the new red and cream livery has been introduced with Nos 10 and 11 entering service, complete with the traditional cream trolley tower. Undoubtedly this was much more attractive and the other OMOs were repainted with red towers, which stood up better to weather than sunshine yellow — as seen here. Of course the striking sign had appeared along the Promenade that year, erected by the Road Safety Committee, to warn pedestrians to avoid walking in front of moving trams. Accidents have happened — including death — because the tramway reservation cannot be fenced in. Pedestrians — don't forget it! *Steve Palmer*

Left: Look out! — this tram is 'Coronation' No 662, one of only four still in service during 1975, which were replaced by OMOs Nos 10–13. The 'Coronations' — here seen in a mundane green and cream livery — were famous in the Blackpool tramway scene during the 1950s and 1960s and popular with the travelling public. However, the safety slogan would apply to the fact that the 'Coronations' — originally equipped with the 'Vambac' equipment — did suffer from electric-brake failure. Thirteen of the original 25 were re-equipped with the standard English Electric controllers, as used in the general fleet, but this reduced their speed. Only No 660 was retained in Blackpool, and can be seen in its original livery to this day. *Steve Palmer*

Above: A historic scene on 12 June 1976, which was the Centenary Day of Blackpool Borough, showing the Promenade Cavalcade watched by the crowds. However, a historic tram has returned to the scene — 'Dreadnought' No 59 — which came from the National Tramway Museum in 1975 and went on static display at Foxhall. This was organised by the Civic Trust, and the body was restored by Blackpool Technical College apprentices, ready for the Borough Centenary.

While it could not take part in the procession, it provided a splendid grandstand for members of the Civic Trust. Subsequently it stayed on in Blackpool until 1990, being a highly popular open-top tram both with tourists and tram enthusiasts. It is now in store at the National Tramway Museum, but may return one day. From this pedestrian bridge we get a delightful view of the 1863 North Pier, which is listed for preservation in its original style. *Steve Palmer*

Above: High Tide on Central Prom in January 1974 as the sea flows over the tram tracks, a boy paddles to safety and the OMOs turn at the Tower. Buses will have replaced the trams to Starr Gate, since the trams cannot achieve earth-return through the track — and they may get water in their motors. In the event of such storms, the trams can be stored at Talbot Square overnight when they can't reach the depot. It is true that the original conduit system of 1885 was adversely affected by the sea and sand, hence the change to the overhead line in 1898. Central Prom and South Shore tend to be prone to flooding when gale-force winds blow along the sea ashore. As shown here, North Pier disappears from view behind the clouds of spray in the air. *Ian McLoughlin*

Above: It is rare that snow provides a white scene at Blackpool, as here at Manchester Square in January 1979. As red OMO No 7 approaches, bound for Starr Gate, it is interesting to note that the Tower is still silver topped following the Queen's Silver Jubilee in 1977. Boats are stored on the Promenade for sailing in the season, but will not be needed just yet! Looking at the track it is apparent that the snow has been ploughed to one side to free the trams for running. Every winter two double-deckers are fitted with ploughs, and they travel along the track during a snow storm to keep it clear. It must be said, however, that snow is unusual in the town and the ploughs are rarely needed. *Ian McLoughlin*

Right: In August 1979, Brush No 638 is seen on the Pleasure Beach loop and it is interesting to recall its experimental conversion to an OMO tram in January 1970. An entrance to the saloon was made behind the driver, with the result that he had to turn round to collect fares. This was not successful, hence the use of English Electric railcoach cars with extended front platforms as OMOs. No 638 was in full-cream livery, but reverted to this livery as a normal two-crew tram with the front entrance sealed. The sliding window to the driver's cab replaced the cab door and No 638 is distinguished by the resistances in the trolley tower. This was its final season in service, and it was withdrawn in May 1980. *Ian McLoughlin*

The Age of the 1980s

Above: A 'new' tram pictured on Central Promenade in 1984, in the form of Glasgow 'Cunarder' No 1297 of 1948, visiting from the National Tramway Museum for the Centenary celebrations in the following year. Undoubtedly its smart livery and handsome appearance commanded the attention of the visitors — especially those from its native Glasgow. I did once hear an English visitor say: 'Look — a new Blackpool tram.' The class of 100 'Cunarders' was nicknamed after the famous liners created at John Brown's shipyard, Clydebank. They had a smarter appearance than the prewar 'Coronations' and had the more modern Maley & Taunton inside-frame bogies, but shared the Metropolitan Vickers electro-pneumatic contactor equipment. No 1297 was rescued from Glasgow, following that city's final tram closure in September 1962, by young enthusiasts (Tony Stevenson and Martin Miller) and arrived at Crich in 1963. For the tram's visit to Blackpool, Sealink sponsored it and advertised on each side. Subsequent to its popular visit, No 1297 returned to Glasgow in 1988 for operation there — in the Garden Festival. Today it resides in the exhibition hall of the National Tramway Museum, until it returns to service again.

Steve Palmer

Right: Pharos Lighthouse in
Fleetwood provides an attractive
setting for Edinburgh No 35,
which arrived here in 1983 from its
native city where it had been
preserved after the system's
closure in 1956. Built at Shrubhill
Works in 1948, No 35 was one of
the last trams to be built,
maintaining the 30ft length and the
four-wheel Peckham P35 truck.
The Edinburgh livery was very
striking in maroon with gold
lining, white roof and flare above
the indicator at each end. Since the
Edinburgh City Tramway layout
was entirely in streets, No 35's
ride over the sleeper-track
reservation in Blackpool gave a
somewhat uncomfortable ride,
with pitching and rolling. No 35
stayed in Blackpool until 1988,
when it went to the Glasgow
Garden Festival for operation,
following which it resided — but
did not operate — at Crich. It is
expected to return to its native city
when Lothian Regional Council
create a museum tram line for its
operation. *Steve Palmer*

Left and below: The last outing for Engineering car No 4 in April 1983 *(left)*, with the men working on the feeder cable at Norbreck. This 1934 works tram had been converted from a 1901 Marton 'Box-car' subsequently rebuilt and lengthened in 1920. It was based at Bispham Depot until the new No 3 arrived in July 1958. Beamish Open Air Museum asked for this tramcar so that they could rebuild it as a traditional open-topper, and it was loaned to them by Blackpool Transport. Considerable expense was involved in rebuilding No 31 to 1920–28 open-top form and it was launched on 17 August 1988, when it emerged in a red and white livery with natural varnished side panels *(below)*. This has become a popular tram at Beamish, but it may return to its native Blackpool for the Centenary celebrations in 1998. *Steve Palmer/Ian McLoughlin*

Left: The arrival of a new tram — 'Centenary' No 641 — at the Depot on 17 April 1984, delivered by a low-loader from East Lancashire Coachbuilders at Blackburn. This was to be the first of a new generation of 10 trams to replace the home-built OMOs of the 1970s. *En route* the prototype 'Centenary' tram was weighed at Whitbread Brewery of Samlesbury near Preston: the body being 9.55 tonnes and the full weight with bogies and equipment 17.29 tonnes. *Steve Palmer*

Right: At Starr Gate on 21 October 1984, the new 'Centenary' car contrasts with 'Coronation' No 660 of the 1950s. The latter class has been phased out of existence. 'Centenary' No 641 has a roof box with the advertisement: 'We are proud of their contribution to 100 years of Transport'. While the new tram rides quite well on its bogies, it has a somewhat squat appearance compared with the 'Coronation'. While the 'Coronations' needed a conductor, the new 'Centenary' cars could operate with a driver only, and this was more economic in staffing. Thus the new tram wins on two points, but definitely not on appearance! *Steve Palmer*

Left: A scenic view at Rossall Farm with 'Dreadnought' No 59 in June 1984, a tram which — as a traditional Promenade open-topper — was rarely seen on the Tramroad. Since its restoration in 1976, the 'Dreadnought' was occasionally used on a market day in the summer weather, when the tourists relished a lovely sightseeing journey. It is worth recording that, in the Tramroad Co days from 1898 to 1919, the track at this point curved to the left and passed close to the gates of Rossall public school. Here was the brick station building which today is repositioned at the present stop next to Rossall Lane crossing. Following the 1920 Blackpool take-over, the line was relocated to its present position in 1924, allowing the creation of Broadway. The original route of the line can still be distinguished, on the edge of Rossall playing field, by the grass embankment. It was there, at a sharp curve, that trams lost their trolleys during gale-force winds, causing a problem for the guards and the stranded passengers. *Steve Palmer*

Right: Manchester 'California' car No 765 is seen in Rossall fields, during a September 1985 tour. In Centenary year, many cities were represented by a tram, including Manchester, whose trams finished in 1949. While all the final trams were scrapped in the yard behind Hyde Road Works, this earlier car survived on a Huddersfield farm. It was brought to Crich by Manchester enthusiasts in 1960, and then taken to Birchfields Road Depot, where it was restored. The bogies came from a Howth tram, No 765 returned to Crich for operation in the 1970s, and then ran at Manchester Heaton Park on a vintage line. In 1985, Blackpool borrowed this attractive tram, and exchanged it for 'Boat' car No 600. While the sun shines upon No 765, storm clouds gathered over Fleetwood, and the driver is wearing his oilskins. The traditional Manchester livery is red and white with beautiful gold lining and insignia on its side, together with the city arms etched upon its glass in the saloon doors. A glorious survival! *Steve Palmer*

Right: At the National Tramway Museum in May 1985 — on Members' Day — when a procession is headed by Blackpool 'Balloon' No 710. During the Centenary year, this tram had been sent in exchange for the historic 'Standard' No 40, which was restored for the occasion. While they are both at Crich on this day, No 40 was subsequently sent to Blackpool for the season, where it became popular again. This view from the bridge shows the procession, including 'Balloon' No 710, 'Standard' No 49, Prague No 180 and Glasgow 'Coronation' No 1282. Visitors have arrived from the car park and are waiting at the tram stop, while the empty bandstand is waiting for its players. Above the quarry is Crich Stand, a memorial to the Sherwood Foresters Regiment. Subsequent to the Tramway Museum Society acquiring the site in 1959, the quarry was reopened, with access for their lorries. While this museum has a large collection of trams, No 710 is back in service on Blackpool Promenade.
Steve Palmer

Left: Pictured on their first appearance together on tour were two products made by Roberts of Horbury — 'Coronation' No 660 of Blackpool and No 513 of Sheffield — in the early 1950s. Charles Roberts & Co Ltd built their first trams for Sheffield in a batch of 35 between 1950 and 1952, which became the final design of four-wheel British double-deckers. Sheffield Queens Road Works built the pioneer No 501 in 1946, a year which marked the jubilee of the City Transport Department. In appearance, while less streamlined, it resembled the 'Baby Grand' Green Goddess of Liverpool, its Maley & Taunton four-wheel truck with 9ft wheelbase together with its two MV-65hp motors, following the tradition of Sheffield because of the hilly terrain. The Blackpool 'Coronations' were built by Charles Roberts from 1952 until 1954, because English Electric — the traditional supplier of trams to Blackpool — had ceased such production having become involved in aviation. The two trams had never appeared together before 1984, when No 513 came from Beamish Museum. Subsequently it returned to Beamish where it still operates to this day, and the 'Coronation' remains in Blackpool.
Steve Palmer

Right: The first Tram Sunday in Fleetwood was on 14 July 1985, when traffic was excluded from Lord Street, vintage buses were exhibited and trams operated as sightseeing transport. The approaching 'Standard' No 40 contrasts with the red Manchester City Transport bus. While No 40 is destined for 'North Station Blackpool', No 4632 is destined for 'Heald Green' — in theory! Looking down Lord Street, many people are free to walk while trams — including Manchester No 765 — travel slowly. Of course this was one of the special events in the Centenary year, but happily the local people wanted to maintain the tradition of Tram Sundays. In 1995, Tram Sunday was opened by the famous Fred Dibnah, who drove his traction engine *Betsy* along Lord Street leading the procession of trams. Since 1985 there have been very few historic trams, but it is hoped that many will return for the Tramroad Centenary in 1998. *Steve Palmer*

Above: A delightful view from the balcony of 'Standard' No 40 in July 1985, looking towards South Pier shows the approaching 'Pantograph' No 167 and illustrates the busy carriageway with many cars. The reservation for the trams distinguishes the unique freedom for Blackpool trams — dating from the widened Promenade of 1905. 'Pantograph' No 167 was on loan from Crich, and had been restored especially for this occasion by the Manpower Services Commission at Bolton. Seen in the postwar livery with Preston McGuire bogies, No 167 does not have the original GEC WT28L 50hp motors. As a works car in 1954, these were replaced by two 35hp BTH B265C, and did not run as fast — but were quieter!

It is well known that the 10 'Pullman' cars No 167–176, were the first Blackpool Borough trams to enter service on the Fleetwood route in 1928, in the red and white livery. They gained their nicknames from the pantographs mounted upon a tall tower, but these lasted only until 1933 when they were replaced by a trolley and the tower shortened. Clearly they retained their name, but their pantographs had been found to spread grease as far as Lytham St Annes and accordingly extend their influence! Apart from this, No 167 is here showing service number '1' on its indicator, and not the Promenade destinations!

Steve Palmer

Right: Centenary Day — 29 September 1985 — with the procession along Central Promenade, led by 1885 car No 4 and followed by 1902 'Dreadnought' No 59, 1924 'Standard' No 40, 1928 'Pantograph' No 167, 'Centenary' No 641, and trams from Edinburgh, Howth, Manchester, Glasgow and Sheffield — a total of 20 trams! The passengers on No 4 are in Victorian costume, including the Mayor and Mayoress, Transport Manager Derek Hyde and his brother Geoff Hyde, TMS President. The crowd in Blackpool on that sunny day was one of the greatest ever — a million strong! *Steve Palmer*

Left: The procession was concluded by a steam tram engine, *John Bull* of 1885, the first time a steam engine had ever appeared on the tramway. It was certainly a contrast to all of the trams, and attracted attention. It had been built by Beyer Peacock of Manchester and exported to Sydney, Australia, displayed, tried, and returned by 1890 to the manufacturer, where it was used as a shunter. It is now at the National Tramway Museum, where it hauls a double-deck trailer tram from Dundee. *Steve Palmer*

Above: The Topless Tour on 4 July 1987 in North Albert Street, Fleetwood, with a unique sight of the three open-top cars together, was organised by Keith Terry. Nearest to the camera is Hill of Howth No 10, which originally operated a scenic route south of Dublin, on a gauge of 5ft 3in. It came to Crich in January 1960, following the closure of the attractive line, and was later restored by Bolton Manpower Workshops for the Blackpool Centenary. It was sponsored by the new Sandcastle at South Shore, whose artistic and colourful advert appears on the decency panels. Notice the high railings around the upper deck — for safety — and the varnished teak livery lined in gold. Along with car No 9, this was built by G. F. Milnes in 1902 and fitted with Peckham Maximum Traction bogies. The other two open-toppers are 'Dreadnought' No 59 and 'Balloon' No 706, the latter having been restored to its original prewar condition for the Centenary year of 1985. It is true that the first 13 of the 'Balloons', Nos 237–249, were open-topped and enclosed by 1942, like the other 14 Nos 250–263. *Steve Palmer*

Above: In complete contrast is this new replica of the former Tramroad Co 'Vanguard' car, numbered 619 and built from OMO No 7 at the workshops in Mode Weel, Salford. This is its first organised tour, on 31 October 1987, and the car is seen in Albert Square, showing its crossbench saloon with a centre aisle. While the principle of introducing a tramroad tradition was intended, it was reminiscent of the MER crossbench cars in the Isle of Man today. However, its appearance was criticised because of its tapered end and incorrect trolley tower of the 1930s,

surmounted by a pantograph. It was felt unsafe to feature the original running-boards which used to reach the crossbench seats, thus there is a perspex screen to contain the passengers. It was expected that other trams of this type would be created from scrapped OMO cars, but No 619 remains unique today. In 1995 the display boards over the saloon sides displayed the forthcoming Centenary in 1998, and it is to be hoped it will appear more correctly traditional by then!
Steve Palmer

Above: A colourful and striking livery of 'Boat' No 606 pictured running on the banks of the River Clyde at the Glasgow Garden Festival, in August 1988. This tramway was created to tour the picturesque site, and the 'Boat' was appropriate in fine weather, along with Paisley No 68, Glasgow Nos 22 and 1297, and Edinburgh No 35. Naturally this was a popular tram …and so was another 'Boat' thousands of miles away! *Steve Palmer*

Right: San Francisco Trolley Festival was operated by MUNI which requested the presence of a Blackpool 'Boat' in 1985. No 603 was given, since it had been loaned to Philadelphia for its Bicentenary in 1976, and retained the 5ft 3in gauge. It crossed the Atlantic again and was restored to the traditional livery, renumbered 228 and fitted with 40 new wooden seats. Joining the international family of trams, the Blackpool 'Boat' operated along the famous Market Street and became very popular with city travellers. In the summer weather they preferred 'sailing' in the 'Boat' rather than descend to the subway and ride on city Boeing articulated trams. Here, No 228 is seen at Bay Bridge Terminal, flying flags — Union Flag, Stars & Stripes, and Skull & Crossbones! *Steve Palmer*

Right: Blackpool & Fleetwood Tramroad Co No 40 was restored to its traditional condition when it returned to Blackpool on 14 June 1988. In 1914, Nos 38–41 were built by the United Electric Car Co of Preston, making a total of 41 trams in the fleet. In 1920, when this car joined Blackpool Corporation fleet, it was renumbered 114 and repainted in the red and white livery. During the 1930s, when the English Electric railcoaches arrived, No 114 became Engineering car No 5, and spent most of the time in Rigby Road Depot where it became a warm staff room. It was restored for the Tramway 75th Anniversary in 1960, and left Blackpool for Crich in April 1963, where it became amongst the first operational trams of 1964. Subsequently it operated in Manchester Heaton Park, where most of the restoration work was completed: body repanelled, repainted, rewired, and wheels retyred. The title, in gold leaf, was painted on the body featuring 'Blackpool & Fleetwood' on each end, but Blackpool Transport required its indicator boxes to be fitted again. In keeping with modern requirements, electric lights are fitted beneath the front frame. Until 1991, No 40 provided an appropriate sight on the coastal line, and with its long wheelbase gave a very comfortable ride. Although it has been stored at Crich, it will doubtless return to celebrate the Centenary of the Tramroad in 1998. *Tony Stevenson*

Above: An historic scene at St Peter's parish church, Fleetwood, while the municipal 'Dreadnought' No 59 and the Company saloon No 40 pose side-by-side, on a tour in May 1990. As you compare the style of each tram, it is clear that the large platform steps and the double staircases of the 'Dreadnought' are appropriate for the mass-loading along the Promenade. However, the high-body of No 40 with the narrow corner entrance and high steps, suit fast-running along the Tramroad with less frequent stops. When the company joined Blackpool Corporation in 1920, the trams like No 40 continued to be used on the Fleetwood line, and less frequently along the Promenade. The survival of these historic trams facilitated their restoration in 1960, but only the 'Dreadnought' was here for the Promenade Centenary in 1985. For the Tramroad Centenary in 1998, No 40 will be in its place but No 59 will not be considered appropriate. However, this view records the meeting of those two trams, in the native territory of No 40! *Steve Palmer*

Above: Bolton No 66 in Albert Square on Tram Sunday — 7 July 1991 — with the Rowntree Clock Tower. No 66 arrived in 1981, following restoration in Bolton by a team led by Derek Shepherd, and provided great interest to the tramway in an age when all its historic trams had departed to museums. The presence of the Bolton tram, restored by enthusiasts, marks the achievement of people from their native town where trams ceased to operate on 29 March 1947. This tram body was found as a chicken coop on a farm and was bought in 1963. In 1972 the correct Brill 21E bogies were bought from Vicinal Museum in Belgium and fitted under the body. A completely new top deck — of a type fitted to the car in 1930 — was built by a specialist using timber from a local Methodist church. In 1979, both halves of the car were moved to Back o' the Bank Power Station at Astley Bridge, where they were fitted out in a workshop. Blackpool's Transport Chairman, Stanley Parkinson, suggested operating vintage trams again — and Bolton No 66 was ready!

Steve Palmer